Editor
Heather Douglas

Illustrator
Kelly McMahon

Cover Artist
Brenda DiAntonis

Editor in Chief
Ina Massler Levin, M.A.

Creative Director
Karen J. Goldfluss, M.S. Ed.

Art Coordinator
Renée Christine Yates

Imaging
Rosa C. See

Publisher

Mary D. Smith, M.S. Ed.

Grade 1

TCR 2911

Paired Passages
Linking Fact to Fiction

Includes Standards & Benchmarks

- Learn to differentiate between nonfiction and fiction.
- Build reading comprehension and critical thinking.
- See how fiction and nonfiction can be connected.
- Synthesize information from two contrasting passages.

Author

Ruth Foster, M.Ed.

Teacher Created Resources, Inc.
6421 Industry Way
Westminster, CA 92683
www.teachercreated.com

ISBN: 978-1-4206-2911-7

© 2009 Teacher Created Resources, Inc.
Made in U.S.A.

Teacher Created Resources

WB

Table of Contents

Introduction 3
Meeting Standards 6
Answer Sheet 7
Paired Passages

Unit 1
Nonfiction: Why the Dog Barked 8
Fiction: The Hot Dog Mystery 9

Unit 2
Nonfiction: Left on the Moon 12
Fiction: Jumping High 13

Unit 3
Nonfiction: The Not Bears 16
Fiction: Only Pizza. 17

Unit 4
Nonfiction: Pockets 20
Fiction: What Aunt Bea Had. 21

Unit 5
Nonfiction: The Island State. 24
Fiction: What Ken Did 25

Unit 6
Nonfiction: Pony in the White House 28
Fiction: The Monster 29

Unit 7
Nonfiction: Dog Food for a Guest 32
Fiction: Where the Hat Could Be 33

Unit 8
Nonfiction: Saved By a Cow 36
Fiction: The Strange Horses 37

Unit 9
Nonfiction: What Covers Most
   of the Earth. 40
Fiction: The Red Sea. 41

Unit 10
Nonfiction: Thumbprints and a Tiger 44
Fiction: The Tiger's Warning 45

Unit 11
Nonfiction: How Louis Could Read 48
Fiction: When the Lights Went Out 49

Unit 12
Nonfiction: What Pulled Andrea Out 52
Fiction: What the Dog Wanted 53

Unit 13
Nonfiction: The Boy Who
   Could Not Sink 56
Fiction: The Floating Egg. 57

Unit 14
Nonfiction: The SKI-DOG 60
Fiction: Help for the Doctor 61

Unit 15
Nonfiction: Drinking Ocean Water 64
Fiction: Letter From a Pen Pal 65

Unit 16
Nonfiction: A Bridge That Is Alive 68
Fiction: The Boat That Was Alive 69

Unit 17
Nonfiction: The Pitcher with One Hand 72
Fiction: The Fast Pitcher 73

Unit 18
Nonfiction: The New Year in China 76
Fiction: The Beast that Ran Away 77

Unit 19
Nonfiction: Growing a Tooth
   in Just One Day 80
Fiction: The Missing Teeth 81

Unit 20
Nonfiction: The United States Flag 84
Fiction: All the Bears 85

Unit 21
Nonfiction: Sailing Across a Continent. 88
Fiction: Seeing Birds that Swim. 89

Unit 22
Nonfiction: What a Camel Can Do. 92
Fiction: Seeing with Closed Eyes 93

Unit 23
Nonfiction: First Across the Channel 96
Fiction: A Swimmer's Diary 97

Unit 24
Nonfiction: A Tongue Twister 100
Fiction: What They Could Eat
   but Could Not Say. 101

Unit 25
Nonfiction: A Country Below Sea Level . . . 104
Fiction: Sarah and the Giant 105

Bibliography 108
Answer Key 110

3/8/10

Introduction

Sometimes new teeth grow back in just one day!

*****

Hoon couldn't because his teeth were missing!

If a student read either one of these statements out of context, it is likely that the student would have a difficult time in knowing which statement was fiction and which one was nonfiction. In addition, the student would have no idea how the two statements could be tied together or used to support an argument or idea.

If, on the other hand, the student read these statements in context and understood how they fit into an entire passage, the student would be able to answer with confidence that it is quite common for some sharks to grow back the teeth they lose in a single day. The student would then be able to compare, contrast, or tie this fact to the passage about a boy whose loose teeth became stuck in an apple he bit into. (Both passages deal with losing teeth.)

Many state tests now contain assessment sections that contain paired passages. After reading two passages, students are expected to differentiate between fiction and nonfiction passages. They are expected to see how the two are connected and understand the underlying connection, as well as how they are dissimilar. They are asked to demonstrate their understanding of the passages by answering multiple choice questions as well as providing written responses.

This is a multileveled task that draws on many different aspects of the reading and writing process. *Paired Passages: Linking Fact to Fiction* was written to provide practice with this type of exercise and assessment, including:

+ exercises that build reading comprehension

+ exercises that develop the skills needed to break down and analyze story elements

+ exercises that provide practice in keeping sequence and details from two sources separate

+ exercises that provide practice in proper letter formation, spacing, and spelling

+ practice with multiple choice questions

+ practice with written response questions on individual passage themes

+ practice with written response questions that utilize information from two contrasting passages

In short, this book was written so that students will develop and practice the skills it takes to compare and contrast fiction and nonfiction passages. If asked, "Is it true that teeth can grow back in just one day?," students will know how to find and use information from two given passages to answer the question. They will also be able to record their reasoned responses in written form.

Using this Book

The Passages

There are 25 units in *Paired Passages: Linking Fact to Fiction.* Each individual unit contains two high-interest passages. The first passage is nonfiction. The second is fiction. Each passage is written at grade level with appropriate vocabulary and sentence structure. The passages are tied together with a common theme. Unit subjects run the gamut from bridges that are alive to burning sea water.

The units may be done sequentially, but they do not have to be. A teacher may choose to go out of order or pick specific units at different times because of class interest or individual students' needs.

Units may be done as a class or assigned as individual work.

The Multiple Choice Questions

A page of multiple choice questions follows the two passages. The first question focuses on the nonfiction passage. The second question focuses on the fiction passage. Answer choices for these questions come only from the passage the question stem is referring to.

The third multiple choice question asks what both passages have in common.

The fourth question requires the student to differentiate between the passages and understand what topic is covered in each one, as the answer choices are drawn from both passages.

Students can answer multiple choice questions on the page by filling in the circle of the correct answer. Students can also answer multiple choice questions by filling in the answer sheet located on page 7. Using this page provides practice responding in a standardized-test format.

Written Responses

A page requiring written responses makes up the final page of each unit. The first written response asks the student to trace and write two new words, one from each passage. This task may appear deceptively simple, but it provides valuable practice and reinforcement of proper letter formation, spacing, and spelling. It is a task that even lower-level or mainstreamed students can engage in.

The following two written responses vary depending on the unit. They may require sequencing of events by filling in boxes, making lists, or even drawing a picture. Each response deals with only one of the passages. They are written to provide students with a foundation of sorting and organizing information. They provide an exercise in referring back to and keeping two different pieces of literary prose separate in the reader's mind.

The last three written responses require higher level responses. First, the students are asked to write out the main theme of each passage with complete sentences. Lastly, they are asked to respond to a question that requires thinking about or using information from both passages to answer.

A teacher's expectations of what is a satisfactory response on these last questions may change over the year, or it may vary depending on the level of the student. For example, at the beginning of the year or with some students, a teacher may accept phonetic spelling and lack of punctuation. As specific topics are covered in class and students become more mature, a teacher may begin to check spelling, capitalization, ending punctuation, etc. Enough variation allows that all students, even those struggling in grade-level writing skills or those with advanced writing skills, can participate.

Meeting Standards

Listed below are the McREL standards used for Language Arts Level 1 (Grades 1–2). All standards and benchmarks are used with permission from McREL. Copyright 2009 McREL. Mid-continent Research for Education and Learning. Address: 4601 DTC Boulevard, Suite 500, Denver, CO 80237. Telephone: 303-337-0990. Website: *www.mcrel.org/standards-benchmarks*.

Uses the general skills and strategies of the writing process

- Uses strategies to organize written work
- Writes in a variety of forms or genres (responses to literature)

Uses the stylistic and rhetorical aspects of writing

- Uses descriptive words to convey basic ideas

Uses grammatical and mechanical conventions in written compositions

- Uses conventions of print in writing
- Uses complete sentences in written compositions
- Uses nouns, verbs, adjectives, and adverbs in written compositions
- Uses conventions of spelling, capitalization, and punctuation in written compositions

Uses the general skills and strategies of the reading process

- Understands that print conveys meaning
- Understands how print is organized and read
- Creates mental images from pictures and print
- Uses meaning clues
- Uses basic elements of phonetic analysis
- Uses basic elements of structural analysis
- Understands level-appropriate sight words and vocabulary
- Uses self-correction strategies

Uses reading skills and strategies to understand and interpret a variety of literary texts

- Uses reading skills and strategies to understand a variety of familiar literary passages and texts
- Knows setting, main characters, main events, sequence, and problems in stories
- Makes simple inferences regarding the order of events and possible outcomes
- Knows the main ideas or theme of a story

Uses reading skills and strategies to understand and interpret a variety of informational texts

- Uses reading skills and strategies to understand a variety of informational texts
- Understands the main idea and supporting details of simple expository information
- Summarizes information found in texts

Answer Sheet

page _____

1. Ⓐ Ⓑ Ⓒ Ⓓ
2. Ⓐ Ⓑ Ⓒ Ⓓ
3. Ⓐ Ⓑ Ⓒ Ⓓ
4. Ⓐ Ⓑ Ⓒ Ⓓ

page _____

1. Ⓐ Ⓑ Ⓒ Ⓓ
2. Ⓐ Ⓑ Ⓒ Ⓓ
3. Ⓐ Ⓑ Ⓒ Ⓓ
4. Ⓐ Ⓑ Ⓒ Ⓓ

page _____

1. Ⓐ Ⓑ Ⓒ Ⓓ
2. Ⓐ Ⓑ Ⓒ Ⓓ
3. Ⓐ Ⓑ Ⓒ Ⓓ
4. Ⓐ Ⓑ Ⓒ Ⓓ

page _____

1. Ⓐ Ⓑ Ⓒ Ⓓ
2. Ⓐ Ⓑ Ⓒ Ⓓ
3. Ⓐ Ⓑ Ⓒ Ⓓ
4. Ⓐ Ⓑ Ⓒ Ⓓ

page _____

1. Ⓐ Ⓑ Ⓒ Ⓓ
2. Ⓐ Ⓑ Ⓒ Ⓓ
3. Ⓐ Ⓑ Ⓒ Ⓓ
4. Ⓐ Ⓑ Ⓒ Ⓓ

page _____

1. Ⓐ Ⓑ Ⓒ Ⓓ
2. Ⓐ Ⓑ Ⓒ Ⓓ
3. Ⓐ Ⓑ Ⓒ Ⓓ
4. Ⓐ Ⓑ Ⓒ Ⓓ

page _____

1. Ⓐ Ⓑ Ⓒ Ⓓ
2. Ⓐ Ⓑ Ⓒ Ⓓ
3. Ⓐ Ⓑ Ⓒ Ⓓ
4. Ⓐ Ⓑ Ⓒ Ⓓ

page _____

1. Ⓐ Ⓑ Ⓒ Ⓓ
2. Ⓐ Ⓑ Ⓒ Ⓓ
3. Ⓐ Ⓑ Ⓒ Ⓓ
4. Ⓐ Ⓑ Ⓒ Ⓓ

page _____

1. Ⓐ Ⓑ Ⓒ Ⓓ
2. Ⓐ Ⓑ Ⓒ Ⓓ
3. Ⓐ Ⓑ Ⓒ Ⓓ
4. Ⓐ Ⓑ Ⓒ Ⓓ

page _____

1. Ⓐ Ⓑ Ⓒ Ⓓ
2. Ⓐ Ⓑ Ⓒ Ⓓ
3. Ⓐ Ⓑ Ⓒ Ⓓ
4. Ⓐ Ⓑ Ⓒ Ⓓ

page _____

1. Ⓐ Ⓑ Ⓒ Ⓓ
2. Ⓐ Ⓑ Ⓒ Ⓓ
3. Ⓐ Ⓑ Ⓒ Ⓓ
4. Ⓐ Ⓑ Ⓒ Ⓓ

page _____

1. Ⓐ Ⓑ Ⓒ Ⓓ
2. Ⓐ Ⓑ Ⓒ Ⓓ
3. Ⓐ Ⓑ Ⓒ Ⓓ
4. Ⓐ Ⓑ Ⓒ Ⓓ

page _____

1. Ⓐ Ⓑ Ⓒ Ⓓ
2. Ⓐ Ⓑ Ⓒ Ⓓ
3. Ⓐ Ⓑ Ⓒ Ⓓ
4. Ⓐ Ⓑ Ⓒ Ⓓ

page _____

1. Ⓐ Ⓑ Ⓒ Ⓓ
2. Ⓐ Ⓑ Ⓒ Ⓓ
3. Ⓐ Ⓑ Ⓒ Ⓓ
4. Ⓐ Ⓑ Ⓒ Ⓓ

page _____

1. Ⓐ Ⓑ Ⓒ Ⓓ
2. Ⓐ Ⓑ Ⓒ Ⓓ
3. Ⓐ Ⓑ Ⓒ Ⓓ
4. Ⓐ Ⓑ Ⓒ Ⓓ

Why the Dog Barked

A person went to the beach. He dug for clams. He put his clams in a bucket. He was going to take the clams home. He was going to cook and eat them.

The person started to leave. A big dog ran up. The dog put its nose right by the bucket. The dog barked. It barked and barked.

The dog was a police dog. The dog was trained to smell clams. The clams in the bucket were not safe! Something in the water had made the clams unsafe to eat. The police dog kept the person from getting sick.

The Hot Dog Mystery

"Mmm! Those hot dogs smell good!" said Sally. Sally's family was having a picnic at the beach. They were cooking hot dogs.

Just then Sally's brother said, "Look up! High in the air there is a hot air balloon!"

Everyone looked up at the hot air balloon. When they looked down, they did not see something. The hot dogs were gone! No one knew where they had gone. It was a mystery.

At the other end of the beach, a lady said, "What is wrong with the dog? He doesn't seem hungry. It is a mystery why he's not hungry."

Show What You Know

Answer the questions on "Why the Dog Barked" and "The Hot Dog Mystery."
You may look back at what you have read if you need to.

1. **The dog barked at the bucket because**

    (A) it was a police dog.

    (B) it smelled the clams in it.

    (C) it wanted to eat the clams.

    (D) it did not want the person to get sick.

2. **Most likely, where did the hot dogs go?**

    (A) Sally ate them.   (C) The lady ate them.

    (B) The dog ate them.   (D) Sally's brother ate them.

3. **What did you read about in both stories?**

    (A) a hungry dog   (C) a dog at a beach

    (B) what a dog ate   (D) a dog that barked

4. **When you don't know why or how something happens, it is a**

    (A) clam.   (C) balloon.

    (B) police.   (D) mystery.

5. **Practice your handwriting. Trace and write.**

    bucket

    mystery

Show What You Know (cont.)

6. **Think about when things happened in the story. Fill in the boxes to show when they happened in the story.**

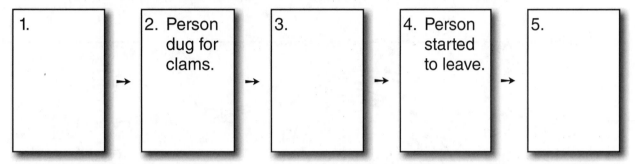

7. **Three people talked in the story "The Hot Dog Mystery." Write down who talked in order.**

1st	
2nd	
3rd	

Write one or more sentences that tell what each story is about.

8. **"Why the Dog Barked"** _____

_____

9. **"The Hot Dog Mystery"** _____

_____

10. **Think of a time when something went missing. Write about what it was. Tell what you think happened to it or about when you found it.**

_____

_____

_____

Left on the Moon

Neil Armstrong stepped out of the *Eagle.* It was July 20, 1969. Neil went where no person had ever gone before. He stepped on the moon.

Neil left something on the moon. He left a flag. A thin wire was sewn on the flag. Why was a thin wire sewn on the flag? The wire held the flag out.

Neil left his footprints on the moon, too. Neil's footprints are still there. Why are Neil's footprints still there? On the moon, there is no wind. There is no rain. Nothing will blow or wash his footprints away.

Jumping High

My name is Luna. I live on the moon. My address is Moon Base 6. I have to wear a space suit outside the station. This is because there is no air on the moon.

I like to jump on the moon. I can jump high. This is because there is less gravity on the moon. People weigh less when there is less gravity.

On the moon, I am very light. I only weigh about 8 pounds (4 kg)! On Earth, I would weigh about 50 pounds (23 kg). It must be very hard to jump on Earth.

Show What You Know

Answer the questions on "Left on the Moon" and "Jumping High."
You may look back at what you have read if you need to.

1. **Why weren't there any footprints on the moon before Neil stepped out of the *Eagle*?**

   Ⓐ Wind had blown away the footprints left before.

   Ⓑ Rain had washed away the footprints left before.

   Ⓒ A flag with a wire was left before, not footprints.

   Ⓓ No person had ever left footprints on the moon before.

2. **Luna can jump higher on the moon than she can on Earth because**

   Ⓐ her space suit makes her weigh less on the moon.

   Ⓑ her space suit makes her weigh more on the moon.

   Ⓒ she weighs less on the moon than she would on Earth.

   Ⓓ she weighs more on the moon than she would on Earth.

3. **Both stories are about**

   Ⓐ being on the moon.   Ⓒ gravity on the moon.

   Ⓑ jumping on the moon.   Ⓓ space suits on the moon.

4. **When Luna plays outside on the moon, she has to make sure she does not**

   Ⓐ jump high.   Ⓒ leave footprints.

   Ⓑ get rained on.   Ⓓ get a rip in her space suit.

5. **Practice your handwriting. Trace and write.**

   footprints

   weigh

14

Show What You Know (cont.)

6. Write the date when the first man took a step on the moon.

_____

Write the year you think people might live on the moon. _____

7. **Fill in the blanks.**

What does Luna like to do? _____

Where does Luna live? _____

When does Luna wear a space suit?_____

Why does Luna weigh less on the moon? _____

Write one or more sentences that tell what each story is about.

8. **"Left on the Moon"**_____

_____

_____

9. **"Jumping High"** _____

_____

_____

10. **Think about if you threw a ball on the moon. Do you think you could throw the ball higher than you could on Earth? Tell why or why not.**

_____

_____

_____

_____

The Not Bears

Some people call koalas "koala bears." The truth is koalas are not bears. Koalas are not like bears at all. Koalas have pouches. Koalas carry their babies in their pouches. Bears do not have pouches.

Koalas live in Australia. They live in trees. People have two thumbs. We have one thumb on each hand. Koalas have four thumbs. They have two thumbs on each hand.

The wind blows. The trees sway. The koalas do not fall out. How do they hold on? How do they stay in the swaying trees? The koalas hold on tight with all their thumbs!

16

Only Pizza

Ben said, "Koalas only eat one thing. They only eat tree leaves. They only eat the leaves of eucalyptus trees. I am going to be like a koala. I am only going to eat one thing. I am only going to eat pizza."

Ben ate pizza for breakfast. He ate pizza for lunch. He ate pizza for dinner. Ben said, "I like being like a koala. I like only eating one thing."

Ben ate only pizza for days. After one week, Ben was sick of pizza. Ben said, "I want an apple! I want rice! I want anything but pizza!"

Show What You Know

Answer the questions on "The Not Bears" and "Only Pizza."
You may look back at what you have read if you need to.

1. **How many thumbs do koalas have?**

   (A) 1   (C) 3

   (B) 2   (D) 4

2. **When did Ben get sick of pizza?**

   (A) after lunch   (C) after one week

   (B) after dinner   (D) after breakfast

3. **What was in both stories?**

   (A) pizza   (C) thumbs

   (B) koalas   (D) leaves

4. **A fact is true. A fact is not made up. "Only Pizza" is a made-up story, but it has a true fact. What answer is a true fact?**

   (A) Koalas only eat eucalyptus leaves.

   (B) Ben likes to eat eucalyptus leaves.

   (C) Koalas like to eat pizza for breakfast.

   (D) Ben has the same number of thumbs as a koala.

5. **Practice your handwriting. Trace and write.**

   pouches

   koala

Show What You Know (cont.)

6. **Look at the hands. Write "koala" or "person" below each hand. Write "thumb" on each thumb.**

1.

_____

2.

_____

7. **Fill in what Ben ate when Ben was acting like a koala.**

breakfast	lunch	dinner

Write one sentence that tells what each story is about.

8. **"The Not Bears"** _____

_____

9. **"Only Pizza"** _____

_____

10. **On the back of this page, write about only eating one thing. When you write,**

- tell what one thing you would most like to eat

- tell how many days you think you could eat one thing and not get sick of it

- tell if you think it would be good for you to eat only one thing like a koala does

Pockets

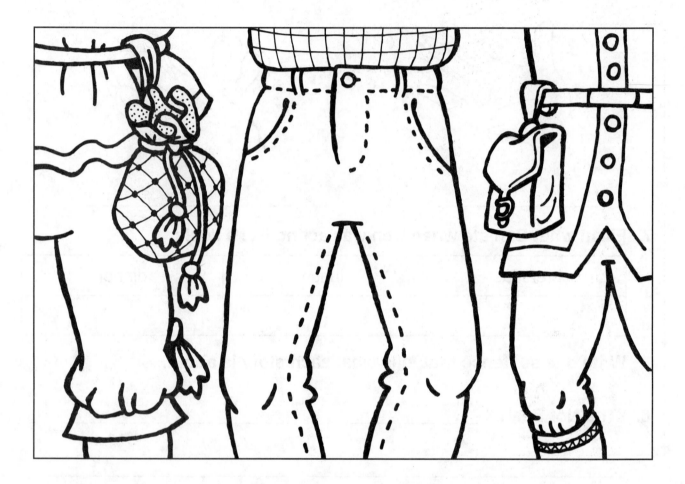

Look at your pants. Are there pockets? Long ago, pants did not have pockets. They were not invented yet. How did people carry things? They used a pouch. The pouch hung from a loop. The loop was on a belt.

When were pockets made? They were invented in the 1600s. The first pockets did not look like today's pockets. The first pockets were like pouches. They hung outside the pants.

When were inside pockets made? They were invented in the 1700s. Today, many pants have pockets. They have lots of pockets. They are inside. They are outside.

What Aunt Bea Had

Aunt Bea said, "Deb, I have a fun riddle for you. It is hard, but it is fun. See if you can answer my riddle."

Deb said, "I like riddles. Ask me your hard, fun riddle."

Aunt Bea said, "I have something in my pocket. I am not carrying anything in my pocket. What is in my pocket if I am not carrying anything?"

Deb said, "That is a hard riddle, but it is a fun riddle. I can answer it. The answer is 'a hole.'"

Aunt Bea said, "Yes, I have a hole in my pocket."

Show What You Know

Answer the questions on "Pockets" and "What Aunt Bee Had."
You may look back at what you have read if you need to.

1. When were inside pockets for pants invented?

(A) in the 1600s   (C) in the 1800s

(B) in the 1700s   (D) in the 1900s

2. Aunt Bea could not carry anything in her pocket because

(A) she had a riddle.   (C) her pocket had a hole.

(B) Deb had something fun.   (D) Deb could answer the riddle.

3. What do both stories have in common?

(A) They both are about pants.   (C) They both are about pouches.

(B) They both are about riddles.   (D) They both are about pockets.

4. From the stories, you can tell that

(A) pockets were invented before riddles.

(B) riddles were invented before pockets.

(C) pockets were invented before pouches.

(D) pouches were invented before pockets.

5. Practice your handwriting. Trace and write.

pockets

riddle

Show What You Know (cont.)

6. **Fill in the chart to show what pockets were like. Write yes or no in each box.**

	inside pockets	outside pockets
1500s		
1600s		
1700s		yes
today		

7. **Write the answer to the riddle:**

   Riddle: What side of a cheetah has the most spots?

   Answer: _____

   (the inside or the outside)

Write one or more sentences that tell what each story is about.

8. **"Pockets"** _____

   _____

   _____

9. **"What Aunt Bea Had"** _____

   _____

   _____

10. **Tell about a pair of pants you have. How many pockets do they have? Where are the pockets? What do you put in the pockets?**

   _____

   _____

   _____

The Island State

Hawaii is a state. It is in the United States. There are 50 states. Hawaii became a state in 1959. It was the 50th state.

Hawaii is made up of islands. The biggest island is the "Big Island." The Big Island is getting bigger. It is growing. How can this be?

There are volcanoes on the island. The volcanoes erupt. Hot lava flows out. The lava cools. It gets hard. It makes new land.

People visit Hawaii. They go to the beach. They lie in the sun. They play. They dig in the sand. They swim. They surf. They fish.

What Ken Did

Ken moved to Hawaii. Megan said, "Ken, I will take you skiing tomorrow."

In the morning, Megan took Ken to the beach. They went water-skiing. Then Megan said, "Get your coat. We are going to ski some more."

Ken said, "Why will I need a coat to ski?"

Megan said, "We are going to ski on snow! We are going to ski down Mauna Kea's slopes. Mauna Kea is a volcano. The top slopes of the volcano are covered in snow."

Ken said, "I like this state! I can ski in two different ways all on the same day!"

Show What You Know

Answer the questions on "The Island State" and "What Ken Did."
You may look back at what you have read if you need to.

1. **Hawaii became a state in**

   Ⓐ 1989.   Ⓒ 1969.

   Ⓑ 1979.   Ⓓ 1959.

2. **What did Megan tell Ken to get?**

   Ⓐ his skis   Ⓒ his slope

   Ⓑ his coat   Ⓓ his volcano

3. **What do both stories have in common?**

   Ⓐ lava   Ⓒ volcanoes

   Ⓑ skiing   Ⓓ becoming a state

4. **From the stories, you can tell that Ken did not know that**

   Ⓐ there was snow in Hawaii.

   Ⓑ Hawaii was the last state.

   Ⓒ there were beaches in Hawaii.

   Ⓓ Hawaii was made up of islands.

5. **Practice your handwriting. Trace and write.**

   island

   volcano

Show What You Know (cont.)

6. **Fill in the boxes to show how the Big Island gets bigger.**

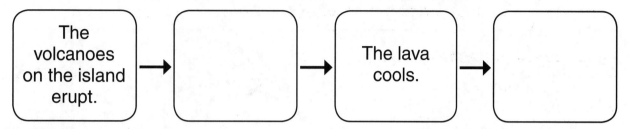

7. **Fill in the chart.**

Way to ski		
Where one can ski this way	beach	
What to wear		

Write one or more sentences that tell what each story is about.

8. **"The Island State"** _____

_____

_____

9. **"What Ken Did"** _____

_____

_____

10. **Would you rather water-ski or snow ski? Tell why. Could you do both on the same day where you live?**

_____

_____

_____

_____

Pony in the White House

Archie Roosevelt was sick. He had to stay in bed. His brothers said, "Archie's pet will make him happy. We will get it."

Archie lived in the White House. He lived there over 100 years ago. He lived there when his father Theodore Roosevelt was President.

Archie's pet was a pony. Archie's brothers sneaked the pony into the White House! They sneaked it into the elevator!

The pony did not want to get out. Why didn't the pony want to get out? There was a mirror in the elevator. The pony did not want to stop looking in the mirror!

28

The Monster

"We can't go up!" said Mato. "There is a real monster up there."

Ron said, "We will be brave. We will go up the stairs. We will go to the top. We won't run away."

The two boys started up the stairs. They went slowly. Then they saw it! It was a monster! It had two heads! The monster was coming closer and closer!

The boys didn't run away. The boys started to laugh. The boys laughed because the monster was not a monster! There was an old mirror at the top of the stairs. The boys were seeing themselves!

Show What You Know

Answer the questions on "Pony in the White House" and "The Monster."
You may look back at what you have read if you need to.

1. **Why didn't the pony want to get out of the elevator?**

   (A) He did not want to stay in bed.

   (B) He did not want to make Archie happy.

   (C) He did not want to stop looking in the mirror.

   (D) He did not want to be sneaked into the White House.

2. **The monster**

   (A) was not old.   (C) was not slow.

   (B) was not real.   (D) was not brave.

3. **What did you read about in both stories?**

   (A) a pony   (B) a mirror   (C) a monster   (D) an elevator

4. **Most likely,**

   (A) the pony did not go up the stairs.

   (B) Mato and Ron sneaked into the White House.

   (C) the pony thought it was seeing a monster with two heads.

   (D) Mato and Ron did not want to stop looking in the mirror.

5. **Practice your handwriting. Trace and write.**

   elevator

   stairs

Show What You Know (cont.)

6. Fill in the blanks.

Archie's pet was a _____.

Archie lived in the _____.

Archie's father was _____.

7. List in order what happened in the story. Use the numbers 1 to 5. Put 1 by what happened first. Put 5 by what happened last.

_____ Ron says, "We won't run away."

_____ The boys know they are looking in a mirror.

_____ The boys see a monster.

_____ Mato says, "There is a real monster up there."

___3___ The boys go slowly up the stairs.

Write one or more sentences that tell what each story is about.

8. "Pony in the White House" _____

_____

9. "The Monster" _____

_____

10. How do you think Archie felt when he saw his pet? Tell why. How do you think Mato and Ron felt when they saw themselves in the mirror? Tell why. _____

_____

_____

Dog Food for a Guest

Jean Craighead George writes books. She writes about animals in a lot of her books. One time, one of Jean's books got a big prize. Jean was excited. She was so excited she did something silly. She meant to give her guest cookies. She gave her visitor dog food instead!

One time, Jean had a small falcon. A falcon is a kind of bird. A falcon eats meat. It hunts small animals. Jean's falcon flew in the house. Where did it land? First, it landed in a bowl of jelly. Then it landed on a guest's head!

Where the Hat Could Be

Morgan said, "Hurry! Hurry! We cannot be late. We don't want to miss the big game. It should be a very exciting game. The Lions and the Falcons are playing."

Scott said, "I am so excited. I just need to find my hat so my head won't get cold while we watch the game. Oh, where could it be? It is not in my room. It is not in the closet. I have looked everywhere! I don't know where it could be."

Morgan looked at Scott. She said, "Scott, you can't see it. It is on your head!"

Show What You Know

Answer the questions on "Dog Food for a Guest" and "Where the Hat Could Be." You may look back at what you have read if you need to.

1. **Where did Jean's falcon land first?**

   Ⓐ on a big prize

   Ⓑ on a guest's head

   Ⓒ in a bowl of jelly

   Ⓓ in a bowl of dog food

2. **In the story, it does not say that Scott looked**

   Ⓐ everywhere.

   Ⓑ in his desk.

   Ⓒ in his room.

   Ⓓ in his closet.

3. **Both stories are about**

   Ⓐ excited people.

   Ⓑ exciting games.

   Ⓒ excited falcons.

   Ⓓ exciting guests.

4. **From the stories, you can tell that**

   Ⓐ Scott was excited to be Morgan's guest.

   Ⓑ Jean would have been excited to go to a game.

   Ⓒ the Falcons are the most exciting team to watch.

   Ⓓ sometimes excited people don't know what they are doing.

5. **Practice your handwriting. Trace and write.**

   guest

   excited

Show What You Know (cont.)

6. **For each group, write 1 or 2 to show what happened first.**

   _____ Jean gave her guest dog food.

   _____ Jean found out her book got a prize.

   -

   _____ The falcon flew in the house.

   _____ The falcon landed on a guest's head.

7. **Write down who said what in the story. Then list in order when it was said. Use the numbers 1 to 4. Put 1 by what happened first. Put 4 by what happened last.**

   _____ "I have looked everywhere."   _____

   _____ "It is on your head.   _____

   _____ "We cannot be late."   _____

   _2_ "I just need to find my hat."   _____Scott_____

   Write one or more sentences that tell what each story is about.

8. **"Dog Food for a Guest"** _____

   _____

   _____

9. **"Where the Hat Could Be"** _____

   _____

   _____

10. **Tell about a time that you were excited. What made you excited? What did you do when you were excited?** _____

    _____

    _____

Saved By a Cow

Don Mottram was on a motorbike. He was looking for a sick calf. Suddenly, Don was hit! An angry bull hit him. The bull knocked Don off his motorbike. It began to step on Don.

Don could not do anything. The bull was too angry and big. Then Don heard a bell. The bell was on Don's lead cow, Daisy. All the other cows followed Daisy and her bell.

Daisy ran to Don. All the other cows followed. Daisy pushed the bull away. Then she and the other cows made a circle around Don. They kept Don safe from the bull.

The Strange Horses

Kim lived in the city. Kim went to the country. She was visiting her friend Betty. Kim saw some animals. The animals were black and white. They said, "Moo."

Kim started to laugh. She said, "Country horses are strange. They do not look like the city horses police officers ride. City horses say 'neigh.' They do not say 'moo'.

Betty started to laugh. She said, "You are not looking at horses. You are looking at cows! The cows are milk cows. The milk you buy in the city comes from cows in the country."

Show What You Know

Answer the questions on "Saved By a Cow" and "The Strange Horses."
You may look back at what you have read if you need to.

1. **What is not true about Daisy?**

   Ⓐ Daisy had a bell.

   Ⓑ Daisy was Don's lead cow.

   Ⓒ The other cows followed Daisy.

   Ⓓ Daisy knocked Don off his motorbike.

2. **Why did Kim go to the country?**

   Ⓐ to buy some milk   Ⓒ to look at some animals

   Ⓑ to visit her friend   Ⓓ to hear a horse say "moo"

3. **What did you read about in both stories?**

   Ⓐ cows   Ⓒ bells

   Ⓑ bulls   Ⓓ horses

4. **From the stories, you can tell that most likely**

   Ⓐ a police officer rode Daisy.   Ⓒ Don lived in the country.

   Ⓑ Betty rode a motorbike.   Ⓓ Kim had seen cows before.

5. **Practice your handwriting. Trace and write.**

   followed

   country

Show What You Know (cont.)

6. **Fill in the chart with the proper names from the story.**

father	
mother	cow
baby	

7. **Complete the chart to show what happened in the story.**

Kim saw some animals she said looked strange.

Write one or more sentences that tell what each story is about.

8. **"Saved By a Cow"** _____

_____

_____

9. **"The Strange Horses"** _____

_____

_____

10. **Think about the different sounds animals make. Think about the different colors animals are. Write down the names of four animals. Write down how they sound. Write down what colors they are.**

_____

_____

_____

_____

_____

What Covers Most of the Earth

What covers most of the Earth? Is it land? Is it water? It is not land. It is water. Ocean water covers most of the Earth.

One ocean is the Pacific Ocean. The Pacific is the biggest ocean. It is the deepest ocean. Lots of islands are in the Pacific Ocean.

One ocean is the Atlantic Ocean. The Atlantic is the second-biggest ocean. Lots of ships cross this ocean.

One ocean is the Indian Ocean. The Indian Ocean is the warmest ocean.

One ocean is the Arctic Ocean. The Arctic is the smallest ocean. It is the coldest ocean.

The Red Sea

Ms. Day said, "The Red Sea is part of the Indian Ocean. Parts of the Red Sea are very hot. How hot are they? They are so hot they can burn your skin!"

Ms. Day's students were surprised. They asked, "What part of the Red Sea is so hot? Why is it so hot?"

Ms. Day said, "Some bottom parts are very hot. They are hot because of volcanic activity. The volcanic activity lets out heat."

"Now," said Ms. Day, "when I drop a blue hat into the Red Sea, what does it become?"

"Wet!" said the students.

Show What You Know

Answer the questions on "What Covers Most of the Earth" and "The Red Sea."
You may look back at what you have read if you need to.

1. **What ocean is the deepest ocean?**

   Ⓐ Arctic Ocean   Ⓒ Pacific Ocean

   Ⓑ Indian Ocean   Ⓓ Atlantic Ocean

2. **The Red Sea is part of what ocean?**

   Ⓐ Arctic Ocean   Ⓒ Pacific Ocean

   Ⓑ Indian Ocean   Ⓓ Atlantic Ocean

3. **What did you read about in both stories?**

   Ⓐ the warmest ocean   Ⓒ the coldest ocean

   Ⓑ the deepest ocean   Ⓓ the biggest ocean

4. **From the stories, you can tell that**

   Ⓐ seas are parts of oceans.

   Ⓑ only blue hats can become wet.

   Ⓒ ships do not cross the Red Sea.

   Ⓓ volcanic activity makes water cold.

5. **Practice your handwriting. Trace and write.**

   _____

   ocean _____

   _____

   volcanic _____

Show What You Know (cont.)

6. List the oceans in order of biggest to smallest. The number 1 is for the biggest ocean. The number 4 is for the smallest ocean.

   1. _____

   2. _____

   3. _____

   4. _____

7. Circle the colors of the hats that would become wet if they were dropped in the Red Sea.

blue	brown	pink
white	red	black
yellow	green	orange

Write one or more sentences that tell what each story is about.

8. "What Covers Most of the Earth" _____

   _____

   _____

9. "The Red Sea" _____

   _____

   _____

10. What ocean is the closest to you? Tell if you think the water is warm enough to swim in all year long.

    _____

    _____

    _____

Thumbprints and a Tiger

Look at your thumb. It has lines on it. These lines are your thumbprint. Thumbprints are not the same. Your thumbprint is your own. No one else has a thumbprint like yours. Your thumbprint tells who you are.

Look at a tiger's face. It has stripes on it. A tiger's face is like your thumbprint. How can a tiger's face be like your thumbprint?

Tiger face stripes are not the same. Each tiger has its own stripe pattern. No other tiger has a stripe pattern like it. A tiger's stripe pattern tells what tiger it is.

The Tiger's Warning

May said, "Look at that tiger's tail. A friendly tiger puts its tail up. It slowly wags it back and forth. That tiger's tail is not up. It is not wagging slowly back and forth."

Lee said, "The tiger's tail is not high. It is low. It is twitching from side to side."

May said, "The tiger is tense. It is telling everyone to be careful. It is warning us to watch our step."

Lee said, "I will tell you something with words, not a tail. I'm glad that tiger is in the zoo and not out here with us!"

Show What You Know

Answer the questions on "Thumbprints and a Tiger" and "The Tiger's Warning."
You may look back at what you have read if you need to.

1. **What is true about a tiger's face stripes?**

   Ⓐ No other tiger has a pattern like it.

   Ⓑ It has the same pattern as other tigers.

   Ⓒ Some other tigers have a pattern like it.

   Ⓓ It has the same pattern as your thumbprint.

2. **A tiger's tail is up high and wagging slowly. The tiger is**

   Ⓐ tense.   Ⓒ telling everyone to be careful.

   Ⓑ friendly.   Ⓓ warning you to watch your step.

3. **What do both stories have in common?**

   Ⓐ They are both about tails.   Ⓒ They are both about tigers.

   Ⓑ They are both about prints.   Ⓓ They are both about patterns.

4. **If Lee ever looked at a tiger's face stripes, Lee would most likely**

   Ⓐ be out with the tiger.

   Ⓑ be looking at its thumbprint.

   Ⓒ be telling people to be careful.

   Ⓓ be looking at a tiger in the zoo.

5. **Practice your handwriting. Trace and write.**

   thumbprint

   tiger

Show What You Know (cont.)

6. **Circle the matching thumbprint and stripe pattern.**

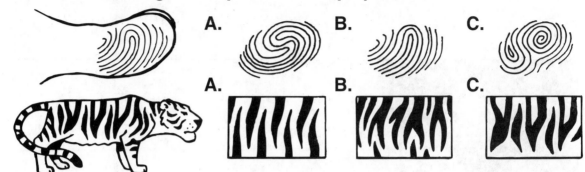

A.   B.   C.

A.   B.   C.

7. **Write down who said what in the story. Then list in order when it was said. Use the numbers 1 to 4. Put 1 by what was said first. Put 4 by what was said last.**

_____ "The tiger is tense."   _____

_4_ "I will tell you something with words."   _____Lee_____

_____ "Look at that tiger's tail."   _____

_____ "It is twitching from side to side.   _____

Write one or more sentences that tell what each story is about.

8. **"Thumbprints and a Tiger"** _____

_____

_____

9. **"The Tiger's Warning"** _____

_____

_____

10. **Think about tigers and people. Write down some things that are the same about tigers and people. Then write down some things that are not the same.** _____

_____

_____

How Louis Could Read

Louis Braille was blind. He could not see. He could not see pages. He could not see letters. Still, Louis could read.

How could Louis read if he could not see pages? How could he read if he could not see letters? How could he read if he could not use his eyes?

Louis could not see the letters, but he could feel them! Louis invented an alphabet. The alphabet was made of dots. Each letter was a different pattern of dots. The dots were raised. Louis could feel the raised dots. Louis could read by using his fingers!

When the Lights Went Out

A big storm hit. Strong winds blew. Trees were knocked over. Zack said, "The power and lights are out. The phone isn't working. It is dark in the house. We cannot watch TV. What can we do?"

Uncle Henry said, "Let's read. I know a good story you will like."

Zack said, "Uncle Henry, I can't read. It is dark."

Uncle Henry said, "I can read to you. My books are printed in the Braille alphabet."

Zack said, "I can't read in the dark, but you can! Uncle Henry, you can read in the dark and the light."

Show What You Know

Answer the questions on "How Louis Could Read" and "When the Lights Went Out." You may look back at what you have read if you need to.

1. **How could Louis read?**

   Ⓐ by using his eyes

   Ⓑ by seeing the pages

   Ⓒ by seeing the letters

   Ⓓ by feeling raised dots

2. **What was not true after the big storm hit?**

   Ⓐ It was dark.

   Ⓑ The phone worked.

   Ⓒ The power was out.

   Ⓓ The lights were out.

3. **What did you read about in both stories?**

   Ⓐ a big storm

   Ⓑ Uncle Henry

   Ⓒ different patterns

   Ⓓ the Braille alphabet

4. **From the stories, you can tell that**

   Ⓐ Zack cannot use his fingers to read.

   Ⓑ Louis did not know any good stories.

   Ⓒ Uncle Henry can see pages and letters.

   Ⓓ Louis read stories when the power was out.

5. **Practice your handwriting. Trace and write.**

   raised

   alphabet

Show What You Know (cont.)

6. **Fill in the blanks.**

   When you read, you use your _____ to _____ the letters.

   When Louis read, he used his _____ to _____ the letters.

7. **Write down who said what in the story. Then, list in order when it was said. Use the numbers 1 to 4. Put 1 by what was said first. Put 4 by what was said last.**

   _____ "I can't read in the dark, but you can!"   _____Zack_____

   _____ "I can read to you."   _____

   _2_ "Let's read."   _____

   _____ "The power and lights are out."   _____

   Write one or more sentences that tell what each story is about.

8. **"How Louis Could Read"** _____

   _____

9. **"When the Lights Went Out"** _____

   _____

10. **Think about if the power, lights, and phone went out in your house. Tell what you could and would do.** _____

   _____

   _____

   _____

What Pulled Andrea Out

Andrea Anderson was playing in the snow. She got cold and started to walk home. A big wind blew her back. The wind blew Andrea into a bank of snow. Andrea was buried! She was buried up to her chest!

Andrea tried to get out. She could not move. She was trapped by the snow. Andrea called for help. No one could hear her. No one could see her.

Only the neighbor's dog Villa heard Andrea. Villa jumped over her fence. She found Andrea. As Andrea held onto Villa's neck, Villa pulled. She pulled and pulled. She pulled Andrea out!

What the Dog Wanted

Juan started down the steep hill. His sled went fast in the snow! Then Juan saw a big dog. The dog was in the way. Juan couldn't stop. His sled was going too fast.

Juan was afraid there was going to be a big crash. He closed his eyes. Suddenly, Juan felt something warm. The big dog was sitting on Juan's lap! It had been knocked onto the sled.

At the bottom of the steep hill, the dog grabbed the sled rope. It started to pull the sled up the hill. The dog wanted to go for another downhill ride!

Show What You Know

Answer the questions on "What Pulled Andrea Out" and "What the Dog Wanted."
You may look back at what you have read if you need to.

1. **How did Andrea get buried up to her chest in the snow?**

   Ⓐ Andrea was playing in a bank of snow.

   Ⓑ Villa pulled Andrea into a bank of snow.

   Ⓒ The wind blew Andrea into a bank of snow.

   Ⓓ Andrea got cold and fell into a bank of snow.

2. **Why didn't Juan stop when he saw the dog?**

   Ⓐ His eyes were closed.　　Ⓒ His sled knocked the dog onto the sled.

   Ⓑ His sled was going to crash.　　Ⓓ His sled was going too fast.

3. **What did you read about in both stories?**

   Ⓐ a dog　　Ⓑ a sled　　Ⓒ a hill　　Ⓓ a wind

4. **From the stories, you can tell that**

   Ⓐ Juan was afraid of getting cold.

   Ⓑ Andrea did not know a dog would help her.

   Ⓒ Juan's sled was stopped by a bank of snow.

   Ⓓ Andrea was sledding before she started to walk home.

5. **Practice your handwriting. Trace and write.**

   buried

   started

Show What You Know (cont.)

6. **Fill in the boxes to show what came before and after in the story.**

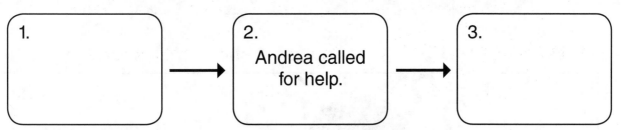

| 1. | | 2. Andrea called for help. | | 3. |

7. **Draw two hills. One hill should be very steep. Draw a sled on the steepest hill.**

Write one or more sentences that tell what each story is about.

8. **"What Pulled Andrea Out"** _____

_____

_____

9. **"What the Dog Wanted"** _____

_____

_____

10. **Think about dogs. Tell how a dog can play or a dog can work. The dog you write about can be a dog you know or a dog you have read about.**

_____

_____

_____

The Boy Who Could Not Sink

A boy jumped into the water. The water was over the boy's head. The boy could not swim. He was not wearing a life vest. The boy did not sink. He could not sink. He floated. How come?

The boy had jumped into the Dead Sea. The Dead Sea is very salty. It is so salty that people cannot sink in it. They float.

The Dead Sea is really a lake. It is a low, salt lake. The Dead Sea is below sea level. Its surface is 1,312 feet (394 m) below sea level. It is in Israel.

The Floating Egg

Jake said, "I can do a magic trick. Watch me, Kelly! Watch me do my magic trick."

Jake picked up an egg. He said, "Watch me while I make this egg float."

Kelly watched as Jake waved his hand over the egg. Then Jake dropped the egg into a glass of water. The egg did not sink! It floated!

Kelly said, "I know you only waved your hand for show. How did you really get the egg to float?"

Jake said, "I added lots and lots of salt to the water."

"That's a good trick!" said Kelly.

Show What You Know

Answer the questions on "The Boy Who Could Not Sink" and "The Floating Egg." You may look back at what you have read if you need to.

1. If you jump into the Dead Sea you cannot

Ⓐ swim.   Ⓑ sink.   Ⓒ float.   Ⓓ wear a life vest.

2. Jake's egg floated because

Ⓐ it was magic.   Ⓒ the water was salty.

Ⓑ Kelly was tricked.   Ⓓ Jake waved his hand.

3. Both stories are about

Ⓐ tricking people.   Ⓒ water that is below sea level.

Ⓑ people who cannot sink.   Ⓓ what happens in very salty water.

4. Oceans are salty. People can sink in the ocean. Most likely, this is because

Ⓐ the ocean is not as salty as the Dead Sea.

Ⓑ Jake did not wave his hand over the ocean.

Ⓒ the Dead Sea is not as salty as the ocean.

Ⓓ Jake did not add lots of salt to the ocean.

5. Practice your handwriting. Trace and write.

salty

float

Show What You Know (cont.)

6. **Circle the word that is wrong in each sentence. Write the correct word.**

The Dead Sea is really an ocean. _____

It is so salty that people can sink in it. _____

Its surface is above sea level. _____

7. **Draw an egg in each glass of water.**

fresh water   **salty water**

Write one or more sentences that tell what each story is about.

8. **"The Boy Who Could Not Sink"** _____

_____

_____

9. **"The Floating Egg"** _____

_____

_____

10. **Do you think you can drink the water in the Dead Sea? Tell why or why not.**

_____

_____

_____

The SKI-DOG

Joseph-Armand Bombardier was born in Canada. He was born in 1907. In the winters, it was very cold. There was lots of snow. The snow was deep. It covered the roads. City roads were plowed. Country roads were not plowed. There were too many roads. There was too much snow.

Country people had to put away their cars. They had to put away their trucks. They had to use sleighs. They had to use horses to pull their sleighs.

Joseph made something. He called it the SKI-DOG. The SKI-DOG could go on unplowed roads. The SKI-DOG was the first snowmobile!

Help for the Doctor

The doctor said, "A farmer is hurt. He needs help. I have to get to him and stitch him up."

The nurse said, "The roads are covered in snow. You will have to go in a sleigh. You will need to hitch your horses to the sleigh."

The doctor said, "I need to get to the farmer fast. I wish there was a better way to get to him."

The nurse said, "Talk to Joseph. He made something that goes across snow fast. It is a snowmobile."

The doctor said, "Doctors help people. A snowmobile can help doctors help people!"

Show What You Know

Answer the questions on "The SKI-DOG" and "Help for the Doctor."
You may look back at what you have read if you need to.

1. **What did country people use in the winter?**

   Ⓐ cars   Ⓑ plows   Ⓒ trucks   Ⓓ sleighs

2. **The doctor needed to hitch up his horses because**

   Ⓐ he had to talk to Joseph.

   Ⓑ the roads were covered in snow.

   Ⓒ the city roads had been plowed.

   Ⓓ it was the better way to get to the farmer.

3. **What did you read about in both stories?**

   Ⓐ a farmer who needed help

   Ⓑ how Joseph made his SKI-DOG

   Ⓒ a new way to get across snow

   Ⓓ what roads were plowed in Canada

4. **From the stories, you can tell that the snowmobile**

   Ⓐ went faster than horses.   Ⓒ could be used to plow roads.

   Ⓑ went slower than horses.   Ⓓ could be hitched to a sleigh.

5. **Practice your handwriting. Trace and write.**

   sleigh

   snowmobile

Show What You Know (cont.)

6. **Fill in the chart to show what things were like in winter.**

	city	country
Roads (plowed or unplowed)		
How people got around		

7. **Write down who said what in the story. Then, list in order when it was said. Use the numbers 1 to 4. Put 1 by what was said first. Put 4 by what was said last.**

   __2__ "You will have to go in a sleigh."   __nurse__

   _____ "Talk to Joseph."   _____

   _____ "I need to get to the farmer fast."   _____

   _____ "I have to get to him and stitch him up."   _____

Write one or more sentences that tell what each story is about.

8. **"The SKI-DOG"** _____

   _____

   _____

9. **"Help for the Doctor"** _____

   _____

   _____

10. **Pretend you live in the country. The roads are covered in snow. Would you like to have a snowmobile? Give two or more reasons why or why not.** _____

   _____

   _____

Drinking Ocean Water

A girl was in Bahrain. Bahrain is a country. The girl had a jar. She walked out into the ocean. She filled her jar. She filled it with water.

What was the water for? The water was for drinking. Ocean water is salty! You cannot drink salty water! How could the water in the jar be for drinking?

In some places, fresh water bubbles up. The fresh water is under the sea bed. The fresh water makes a pocket. It makes a pocket of fresh water in salty water. The water in the jar was not salty. It was fresh.

Letter From a Pen Pal

Dear Franklin,

Long ago, people in my country used wax. They put the wax in their ears! I will tell you why. The people were divers. They dove deep into the ocean. They used the wax to protect their ears.

What were the people diving for? I will tell you. They were diving for pearls. It was dangerous to dive for pearls. The divers had to watch out for sharks. They had to watch out for sea snakes. They had to watch out for jellyfish.

Please tell me what people did in your country.

Your pen pal from Bahrain,

Ali

Show What You Know

Answer the questions on "Drinking Ocean Water" and "Letter From a Pen Pal."
You may look back at what you have read if you need to.

1. **Where did the fresh water come from?**

   (A) under the sea bed   (C) under the sea bubble

   (B) under the salt bed   (D) under the salt bubble

2. **It did not say in the story that the divers had to watch out for**

   (A) sharks.   (C) jellyfish.

   (B) stingrays.   (D) sea snakes.

3. **Both stories are about**

   (A) diving.   (C) Bahrain.

   (B) pearls.   (D) fresh water.

4. **From the stories, you can tell that most likely**

   (A) the divers drank the pearls.

   (B) the girl with the jar used wax.

   (C) the girl used her jar for pearls.

   (D) the divers dove mainly in salty water.

5. **Practice your handwriting. Trace and write.**

   water

   pearls

Show What You Know (cont.)

6. **Look at a map. Find Bahrain. Answer the questions.**

   • Is your country bigger or smaller than Bahrain? _____

   • Is your country as close to an ocean as Bahrain? _____

   • Where do you get fresh water in your country? _____

7. **A letter has a greeting. It has a closing. Write down the greeting and the closing of Ali's letter. Remember your commas. A comma looks like this: ,**

   Greeting:_____

   Closing: _____

Write one or more sentences that tell what each story is about.

8. **"Drinking Ocean Water"**_____

   _____

   _____

9. **"Letter from a Pen Pal"** _____

   _____

   _____

10. **Ali asked Franklin to please tell him what people did in his country. Pretend you are Ali's pen pal. On the back of this paper, write Ali a letter. Tell him something that people did long ago in your country. Remember to put a greeting and a closing in your letter.**

A Bridge That Is Alive

Deep in the jungle, ants are marching. The ants are army ants. The army ants are looking for food. The ants come to a place that they cannot cross. What can the ants do to get across?

Some of the ants link their legs together. They make a chain. The chain is strong. It stretches to the other side. The chain makes a bridge that is alive! It is a bridge made up of army ants!

Other ants walk across the chain. They cross to the other side. Then they continue to march. They keep on marching deep in the jungle.

A Bridge That Is Alive

Max visited the rainy jungle. The ground was flooded. Water was everywhere. Max saw something strange. It was floating in the water.

"Don't touch it!" cried Max's guide. "That floating thing is alive!"

Max was puzzled. What could the strange thing be?

The guide said, "It is a bunch of ants. The ants have joined together so they are like an 'ant boat.' As the 'boat' floats, it rolls over and over. The ants go in and out of the water. The 'boat' keeps them from drowning. They do not drown because they breathe when they roll out of the water."

Show What You Know

Answer the questions on "A Bridge That Is Alive" and "The Boat That Was Alive."
You may look back at what you have read if you need to.

1. **The ants make a chain by**

   Ⓐ continuing to march.   Ⓒ linking their legs together.

   Ⓑ marching deep in the jungle.   Ⓓ stretching to the other side.

2. **A guide**

   Ⓐ is a bunch of ants.   Ⓒ is a boat that is alive.

   Ⓑ shows visitors around.   Ⓓ joins visitors together.

3. **What did you read about in both stories?**

   Ⓐ ants   Ⓒ chains

   Ⓑ boats   Ⓓ bridges

4. **Most likely, the ants make an 'ant boat'**

   Ⓐ when they are puzzled.

   Ⓑ when they are looking for food.

   Ⓒ when they want to cross the jungle.

   Ⓓ when the jungle floods so they do not drown.

5. **Practice your handwriting. Trace and write.**

   chain

   floating

Show What You Know (cont.)

6. **Circle what ants have their legs linked together.**

   A.

   B.

   C.

7. **Fill in the boxes.**

Why the ants are like a real boat.	Why the ants are not like a real boat.

Write one or more sentences that tell what each story is about.

8. **"A Bridge That Is Alive"** _____

   _____

   _____

9. **"The Boat That Was Alive"** _____

   _____

   _____

10. **Think about some ants you have seen. On the back of this paper, write about the ants. Tell what they looked like. Tell what they were doing. Or, write about a bridge you have seen. Tell where the bridge is. Tell what it is for and what it is made of.**

The Pitcher with One Hand

Jim Abbot was born with only one hand. Kids were mean to Jim. They called him names. Jim wanted to play baseball. He did not care if he only had one hand.

People said, "You won't go far." Jim didn't listen. He practiced. He practiced pitching with his one hand. He practiced throwing with his one hand. He practiced slipping his glove on and off.

Jim's practice paid off. Jim became a great baseball star. He went to the Olympics. He earned a gold medal. Then he turned pro. Jim had a missing hand, but he helped his teams win!

72

The Fast Pitcher

Tim was watching a baseball game. "Dad," said Tim in surprise, "the pitcher is one-handed! How can he pitch, catch, and throw?"

Tim's dad said, "That's Jim Abbot. Watch how he does it."

Tim saw Jim pitch with his left hand. Jim held his glove in the crook of his right elbow. Jim slipped the glove on his left hand after pitching.

Tim saw Jim catch a ball. Jim cradled the glove and ball in the crook of his right elbow. He grabbed the ball with his left hand and threw it.

Tim said, "He's not just one-handed! He's fast!"

Show What You Know

Answer the questions on "The Pitcher with One Hand" and "The Fast Pitcher."
You may look back at what you have read if you need to.

1. **How did Jim become such a good baseball player?**

   Ⓐ He practiced.   Ⓒ He earned a gold medal.

   Ⓑ He turned pro.   Ⓓ He helped his teams win.

2. **When Jim pitched, where did he hold his glove?**

   Ⓐ in his left hand

   Ⓑ in his right hand

   Ⓒ in the crook of his left elbow

   Ⓓ in the crook of his right elbow

3. **What do both stories have in common?**

   Ⓐ mean kids   Ⓒ the Olympics

   Ⓑ a pitcher   Ⓓ Tim and his dad

4. **Most likely, Jim helped his teams win because**

   Ⓐ he went far.   Ⓒ he was fast.

   Ⓑ he listened.   Ⓓ he was one-handed.

5. **Practice your handwriting. Trace and write.**

   practiced

   glove

Show What You Know (cont.)

6. **What three things did Jim practice?**

   1. _____

   2. _____

   3. slipping his glove on and off_____

7. **Write down if the hand is the left or the right.**

   _____ _____ _____ _____

Write one or more sentences that tell what each story is about.

8. **"The Pitcher with One Hand"** _____

   _____

   _____

9. **"The Fast Pitcher"** _____

   _____

   _____

   _____

10. **Think of something you can do. Perhaps it will be riding your bike, tying your shoe, writing your name, or jumping. How long did you have to practice at it before you could do it? What would happen if you practiced it even more?**

    _____

    _____

    _____

The New Year in China

China is a country. It is a big country. People in China celebrate. They celebrate the New Year. When is the New Year? It is when a new moon comes. It is between January 21 and February 19.

People are happy. They eat good food. They play games. They have fun. They talk. They laugh. They set off firecrackers.

The New Year has a color. The color is red. People wear red clothes. They hang up red papers. They paint their doors red. The color red is everywhere. Red is the color of the New Year.

The Beast that Ran Away

A bad beast came at the end of every year. It came to villages in China. The beast did bad things. It ate the villager's animals. The villagers fought the beast, but it always came back.

The villagers found out something. They found out the beast did not like light. It did not like noise. It did not like the color red.

At the end of the year, the villagers lit a big bonfire. They lit lots of firecrackers. They painted the doors of their homes red. The beast was scared by the light, noise, and red doors. It ran away.

Show What You Know

Answer the questions on "The New Year in China" and "The Beast that Ran Away." You may look back at what you have read if you need to.

1. **The New Year is between**

   Ⓐ January 12 and February 19. Ⓒ January 21 and February 19.

   Ⓑ January 19 and February 21. Ⓓ January 21 and February 21.

2. **What was not true about the beast?**

   Ⓐ It lit lots of firecrackers. Ⓒ It ate the villager's animals.

   Ⓑ It did not like the color red. Ⓓ It came at the end of every year.

3. **What did you read about in both stories?**

   Ⓐ a big beast Ⓒ the color red

   Ⓑ the new moon Ⓓ a bad country

4. **Most likely, red is the color of the New Year because**

   Ⓐ firecrackers make a lot of noise.

   Ⓑ people painted the doors of their homes red.

   Ⓒ the New Year comes when there is a new moon.

   Ⓓ it is said that the color red scared the beast.

5. **Practice your handwriting. Trace and write.**

   celebrate

   villagers

Show What You Know (cont.)

6. **List the six things it says in the story that people do to celebrate the New Year.**

   1. ___eat good food___   4. _____

   2. _____   5. _____

   3. _____   6. _____

7. **Fill in the chart. Tell what the villagers did when they found out that the beast did not like the following:**

light	
noise	
red	

Write one or more sentences that tell what each story is about.

8. **"The New Year in China"** _____

   _____

   _____

9. **"The Beast that Ran Away"** _____

   _____

   _____

10. **Think of when you celebrate the New Year. When do you celebrate it? How do you celebrate it?** _____

    _____

    _____

Growing a Tooth in Just One Day

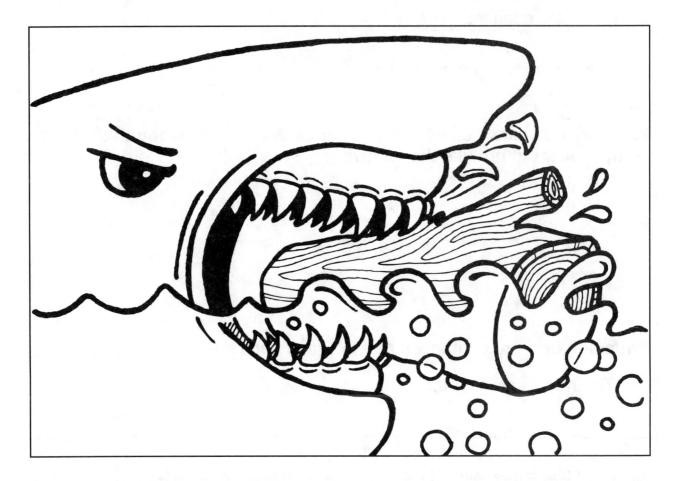

Sharks have lots of sharp teeth. Sharks have powerful jaws. With their sharp teeth and powerful jaws, sharks can bite hard. They can bite through steel!

Sharks lose their teeth all the time. Their teeth fall out every time they bite something hard. You don't lose teeth all the time. You only lose your baby teeth. This is because your teeth are set firmly into your jaw. A shark's teeth are not set firmly in its jaw.

Your teeth take a long time to grow in. Shark teeth grow in fast. Sometimes new teeth grow back in just one day!

The Missing Teeth

Hoon had two loose teeth. Hoon would wiggle his teeth with his tongue. He wiggled his teeth back and forth for three days.

On the fourth day, Hoon bit into a hard apple. After his first bite, Hoon tried to wiggle his teeth with his tongue. Hoon couldn't because his teeth were missing!

Hoon yelled, "Help! Help! My teeth are gone!"

Hoon's father and sister came running. They looked in Hoon's mouth. They looked on the floor. They could not find the missing teeth. Then Hoon's sister said, "Hoon, look at your apple. Your teeth are stuck in the apple!"

Show What You Know

Answer the questions on "Growing a Tooth in Just One Day" and "The Missing Teeth." You may look back at what you have read if you need to.

1. **What is true about shark teeth?**

   Ⓐ They are not sharp.

   Ⓑ The do not grow in fast.

   Ⓒ They do not fall out easily.

   Ⓓ They are not set firmly in the jaw.

2. **How many loose teeth did Hoon have?**

   Ⓐ 1   Ⓒ 3

   Ⓑ 2   Ⓓ 4

3. **Both stories are about**

   Ⓐ jaws.   Ⓒ sharks.

   Ⓑ teeth.   Ⓓ apples.

4. **Most likely, if something is firmly set,**

   Ⓐ it can wiggle.   Ⓒ it cannot wiggle.

   Ⓑ it can bite hard.   Ⓓ it cannot bite hard.

5. **Practice your handwriting. Trace and write.**

   teeth

   tongue

Show What You Know (cont.)

6. **Fill in the boxes. Tell how your teeth are the same or different from shark teeth.**

	Shark	You
How many teeth? more/less		
How sharp? more/less		
How long to grow in? faster/slower/same		

7. **Tell something that happened before.**

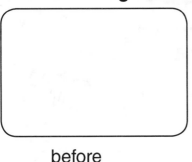

Hoon took a bite of apple.

before   after

Write one or more sentences that tell what each story is about.

8. **"Growing a Tooth in Just One Day"** _____

   _____

9. **"The Missing Teeth"** _____

   _____

10. **On the back of this paper, write about your teeth. Tell how many are loose. Tell how many you have lost. Tell how you lost them. Tell what you did with your baby teeth. If you have not lost any teeth, tell when, where, and how you think you will lose them. Tell what you will do with them.**

The United States Flag

The United States has a flag. The flag has stars. It has 50 stars. The stars are white. The stars are on a field of blue.

The flag has stripes. It has 13 stripes. Some stripes are red. Some stripes are white.

Why does the flag have 50 stars? The United States is a big country. It is made up of 50 states. Each star stands for one state.

Why does it have 13 stripes? Long ago, the United States did not have 50 states. It was a much smaller country. The 13 stripes stand for the first states.

All the Bears

Kit said, "Jill, let's count. Let's count the grizzly bears we see today."

All day, Kit and Jill looked for grizzly bears. They kept count of all the bears they saw. One bear was in front of the school. One bear was in front of the police station. One bear was in front of the fire station. One bear was in front of the library.

How could there be bears in front of the school and library? How could there be bears in front of the police station and fire station? The grizzly bears were on the California state flag!

Show What You Know

Answer the questions on "The United States Flag" and "All the Bears."
You may look back at what you have read if you need to.

1. **What is not true about the stripes on the United States flag?**

   Ⓐ There are 13 stripes.   Ⓒ There are blue stripes.

   Ⓑ There are red stripes.   Ⓓ There are white stripes.

2. **How many grizzly bears did Kit and Jill count?**

   Ⓐ 3   Ⓒ 5

   Ⓑ 4   Ⓓ 6

3. **Both stories are about**

   Ⓐ bears.   Ⓒ flags.

   Ⓑ stars.   Ⓓ stations.

4. **From the stories, you can tell that**

   Ⓐ grizzly bears are on all flags.

   Ⓑ only California has a state flag.

   Ⓒ all flags are red, white, and blue.

   Ⓓ state flags are not the same as country flags.

5. **Practice your handwriting. Trace and write.**

   stripes

   grizzly

Show What You Know (cont.)

6. **Think about what the United States flag looks like. Fill in the boxes.**

	color	how many?
stars		
field		
stripes		

7. **List the places Kit and Jill saw the California state flag.**

    1. _____   3. _____

    2. _____   4. _____

Write one or more sentences that tell what each story is about.

8. **"The United States Flag"** _____

    _____

    _____

9. **"All the Bears"** _____

    _____

    _____

10. **On the back of this page, draw a picture of or write about a state or country flag. Make sure you write what country or state your flag is from.**

Sailing Across a Continent

Antarctica is a continent. It is the emptiest continent. This is because it is so cold. There is so much ice.

Borge Ousland was all alone. He crossed Antarctica. No one had ever crossed Antarctica alone before. It was too cold. It was too far. There was no one to help on the way.

How did Borge cross? He used skis. He pulled a sled. He also had sails! He tied the sails to his body. The sails would fill with air. They helped him go fast. The sails helped him pull his heavy sled.

Seeing Birds that Swim

Ryan said, "There is a bird that cannot fly. The bird cannot fly, but it can swim. Some of these birds stay in the water for a long time. They stay in the water for five months!"

Jon said, "Where can I see a bird like that?"

Ryan said, "These birds live in Antarctica. I will take you to see one."

Jon said, "You can't take me to Antarctica!"

Ryan said, "I can't take you to Antarctica, but I can take you to the zoo! We will see penguins at the zoo. We will see penguins from Antarctica."

Show What You Know

Answer the questions on "Sailing Across a Continent" and "Seeing Birds that Swim." You may look back at what you have read if you need to.

1. **What did Borge do that no one else had ever done before?**

   Ⓐ He crossed Antarctica alone.

   Ⓑ He used skies to go fast on ice.

   Ⓒ He pulled a heavy sled in the cold.

   Ⓓ He tied sails that would fill with air to his body.

2. **How long do some penguins stay in the water?**

   Ⓐ 2 months   Ⓒ 4 months

   Ⓑ 3 months   Ⓓ 5 months

3. **What did you read about in both stories?**

   Ⓐ ice   Ⓑ sails   Ⓒ penguins   Ⓓ Antarctica

4. **From the stories, you can tell that Borge**

   Ⓐ could have swum across Antarctica.

   Ⓑ could have seen penguins in Antarctica.

   Ⓒ could have gone to the zoo in Antarctica.

   Ⓓ could have talked to Ryan about Antarctica.

5. **Practice your handwriting. Trace and write.**

   continent

   Antarctic

Show What You Know (cont.)

6. **List why no one had crossed Antarctica alone before.**

   1. _____

   2. It was too far. _____

   3. _____

7. **Write down who said what in the story. Then, list in order when it was said. Use the numbers 1 to 5. Put 1 by what was said first. Put 5 by what was said last.**

   _____ "You can't take me to Antarctica!"   _____

   _____ "Where can I see a bird like that?"   _____

   _____ "There is a bird that cannot fly."   _____

   _____ "We will see penguins at the zoo."   _____

   __3__ "I will take you to see one."   _____ Ryan _____

Write one or more sentences that tell what each story is about.

8. **"Sailing Across a Continent"** _____

   _____

   _____

9. **"Seeing Birds that Swim"** _____

   _____

   _____

10. **If you went to the zoo, what would you want to see? Tell what continent the animal comes from. Tell why it would be easier for you to see this animal in the zoo than in the wild.**

   _____

   _____

   _____

What a Camel Can Do

Camels live in the desert. Sometimes there are storms in the desert. The storms are not rainstorms. They are not snowstorms. They are sandstorms.

Sand blows everywhere. It fills the air. Sand will blow into a person's nose. Sand will not blow into a camel's nose! Why won't sand blow into a camel's nose?

A camel can close up its nose! It can shut its nostrils. It can close its nostrils so sand cannot blow in.

Seeing with Closed Eyes

Kay shut her eyelids. She tried to walk. Kay could not see. She kept bumping into things. She had to open her eyes.

Kay said, "A camel can close its eyelids. It can still see. It can still walk. Why can't I?"

Alex said, "Kay, you are not a camel! You are a girl! People only have two eyelids for each eye, the upper and lower. Camels have three eyelids for each eye. One eyelid is very thin. It is so thin a camel can see through it. A camel closes this eyelid during a sandstorm. The camel can still see, but its eye is safe from the sand."

Show What You Know

Answer the questions on "What a Camel Can Do" and "Seeing with Closed Eyes." You may look back at what you have read if you need to.

1. **What kind of storm is not in the story "What a Camel Can Do"?**

   (A) sandstorm   (C) snowstorm

   (B) rainstorm   (D) hailstorm

2. **How many eyelids does a camel have?**

   (A) 1   (C) 3

   (B) 2   (D) 4

3. **Both stories are about**

   (A) camels.   (C) eyelids.

   (B) deserts.   (D) nostrils.

4. **From the stories, you can tell that**

   (A) camels have ways to be safe in sandstorms.

   (B) camels have more nostrils than people have.

   (C) a camel can see when all of its eyelids are closed.

   (D) camels do not bump into things when they are walking.

5. **Practice your handwriting. Trace and write.**

   nostrils

   eyelid

Show What You Know (cont.)

6. Write in the right number.

How many noses do you have? _____

How many nostrils do you have? _____

How many nostrils can you close? _____

7. List in order what Kay does in the story. Use the numbers 1 to 5. Put 1 by what happened first. Put 5 by what happened last.

_____ asked how camels see   _____ found out about a thin eyelid

_____ bumped into things   _____ opened her eyes

_____ shut her eyes

Write one or more sentences that tell what each story is about.

8. "What a Camel Can Do" _____

_____

_____

9. "Seeing with Closed Eyes" _____

_____

_____

10. Pretend that you are going to the desert. You want to be safe in a sandstorm. What should you bring and why? Make sure you talk about your eyes and your nose in your answer. _____

_____

_____

First Across the Channel

The wind was strong. The water was choppy. Ships were told, "You cannot cross. The wind is too strong. The water is too choppy. You cannot cross the channel."

Gertrude Ederle was in the water. She was swimming the channel. She was swimming from France to England. Gertrude's trainer was in a boat. He wanted to be safe. He told Gertrude she had to get out of the water.

Gertrude said, "What for?" Gertrude stayed in the choppy water! She did not stop swimming. She swam across the channel. She was the first woman to swim from France to England.

A Swimmer's Diary

August 5, 2008

Dear Diary,

Tomorrow, I will try to swim across the channel! At last, I will try to do what my hero did. Gertrude is my hero. She was the first woman to swim across the channel. She swam it on August 6 in 1926.

I will be like Gertrude. I will coat my skin with lard. Lard is fat. The lard will help me stay warm. It will help protect me from the icy water.

August 6, 2008

Dear Diary,

I did it! I swam from France to England! I swam across the channel like my hero!

Show What You Know

Answer the questions on "First Across the Channel" and "A Swimmer's Diary."
You may look back at what you have read if you need to.

1. **Why did Gertrude's trainer tell Gertrude she had to get out of the water?**

   Ⓐ He wanted to be safe.

   Ⓑ He wanted Gertrude to be first.

   Ⓒ He wanted to be Gertrude's trainer.

   Ⓓ He wanted to go from France to England.

2. **How many days in the swimmer's diary did you read about?**

   Ⓐ 1   Ⓑ 2   Ⓒ 3   Ⓓ 4

3. **Both stories are about**

   Ⓐ Gertrude's diary.   Ⓒ what Gertrude said.

   Ⓑ how to stay warm.   Ⓓ swimming the channel.

4. **Most likely, Gertrude did not wear a wet suit to stay warm because**

   Ⓐ wet suits had not been invented yet.

   Ⓑ her trainer told her to use a wet suit.

   Ⓒ she knew later swimmers would want to use lard.

   Ⓓ wet suits protect against icy water better than lard.

5. **Practice your handwriting. Trace and write.**

   channel

   diary

Show What You Know (cont.)

6. **Fill in the boxes to show what came before and after in the story.**

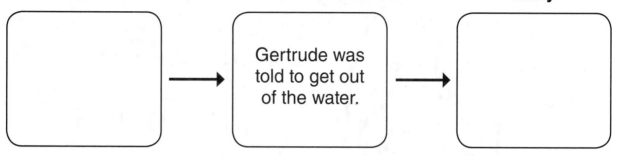

Gertrude was told to get out of the water.

7. **A diary has dates in it. Write down one of the dates from the story "A Swimmer's Diary."**

_____

Now, put a circle around the month.

Put a box around the day of the month.

Put a line under the year.

Write one or more sentences that tell what each story is about.

8. **"First Across the Channel"** _____

_____

_____

9. **"A Swimmer's Diary"** _____

_____

_____

10. **Write a note for your diary. In your note, tell about a hero you have. Tell about something you would like to do like your hero. Be sure and start your diary note with today's date.**

_____

_____

_____

A Tongue Twister

You can read the words "toy" and "boat." It is easy to say each word. It is easy to say each word fast.

Now try to say the words together. Try to say them together five times fast!

toy boat

toy boat

toy boat

toy boat

toy boat

Most likely, you could not do it. Your sounds did not come out right.

Together, the words "toy" and "boat" make up a tongue twister. Tongue twisters are words you cannot say over and over fast. If you try, your tongue will feel like it is all twisted up!

What They Could Eat but Could Not Say

Claire said, "Try and say, 'a box of biscuits' five times as fast as you can. I do not think you can. I think you will make a mistake."

Henry tried. He made many mistakes. Henry said, "Now it is your turn. Try and say, 'She sells seashells by the seashore' five times fast."

Claire and Henry both tried to say the tongue twisters. They laughed at their mistakes. Claire said, "Let's stop. Let's go eat fresh figs and cheap sheep soup."

Henry said, "We can eat fresh figs and cheap sheep soup, but we can't say them fast!"

Show What You Know

Answer the questions on "A Tongue Twister" and "What They Could Eat but Could Not Say." You may look back at what you have read if you need to.

1. **The words "toy" and "boat" make up a tongue twister**

   Ⓐ when you say each word fast.

   Ⓑ when you say each word over.

   Ⓒ when you say the words and they sound right.

   Ⓓ when you say the words together quickly many times.

2. **What did Henry and Claire do when they made mistakes?**

   Ⓐ laughed   Ⓒ twisted their tongues

   Ⓑ ate fresh figs   Ⓓ stopped to get biscuits

3. **What did you read about in both stories?**

   Ⓐ toy boats   Ⓒ cheap sheep

   Ⓑ word sounds   Ⓓ fast tongues

4. **What answer, if you say it fast, is a tongue twister?**

   Ⓐ short, short, short, short

   Ⓑ swords, swords, swords, swords

   Ⓒ short swords, short swords, short swords

   Ⓓ big swords, big swords, big swords, big swords

5. **Practice your handwriting. Trace and write.**

   together

   mistake

Show What You Know (cont.)

6. Draw two lines. One line should be straight. One line should be twisted. Write the word "twisted" under the line that is twisted.

7. Say the words below five times fast. Which ones are tongue twisters?

	Yes or No
fresh	
fresh figs	
cheap	
sheep soup	
cheap sheep soup	

Write one or more sentences that tell what each story is about.

8. "A Tongue Twister" _____

_____

_____

9. "What They Could Eat but Could Not Say" _____

_____

_____

10. Make up a tongue twister. It can be long or short. If you want, you may use some of these words: *fries, flies, fruit, fresh, free*

_____

_____

_____

A Country Below Sea Level

The Netherlands is a country. Much of the land is flat. It is low. It is below sea level. The Netherlands is close to the sea. Why isn't the land under water? Why isn't the land flooded?

People in the Netherlands made dikes. A dike is a kind of dam. The dikes in the Netherlands are like low walls.

First, the people built dikes around an area. They built canals, too. Then the people pumped out the sea water from the land inside the dikes. The sea water ran through the canals. It ran back into the ocean.

Sarah and the Giant

A mean giant dumped a huge pile of dirt in the river. The dirt made a dam. The dam stopped the water.

The giant roared, "I am big and strong! You can't move all that dirt! You will never get water to your village!"

Sarah said, "I can get the water to go to my village." Sarah took a little spoon. She dug a tiny gap across the top of the dam. Water began to flow slowly through the gap. Then it began to flow faster and stronger.

Sarah said, "I am small and weak, but I can think."

Show What You Know

Answer the questions on "A Country Below Sea Level" and "Sarah and the Giant." You may look back at what you have read if you need to.

1. **What is not true about land in the Netherlands?**

    Ⓐ It is low.

    Ⓑ It is flat.

    Ⓒ It is flooded.

    Ⓓ It is below sea level.

2. **Sarah did not have to move all the dirt because**

    Ⓐ the dam was tiny.

    Ⓑ she was small and weak.

    Ⓒ she only had a little spoon.

    Ⓓ the water flowed through a gap.

3. **What did you read about in both stories?**

    Ⓐ dams

    Ⓑ giants

    Ⓒ canals

    Ⓓ sea water

4. **A gap in a dike would**

    Ⓐ pump out sea water.

    Ⓑ let sea water flood the land.

    Ⓒ make the Netherlands into a pile of dirt.

    Ⓓ stop sea water from flowing into the canals.

5. **Practice your handwriting. Trace and write.**

    canals

    dirt

Show What You Know (cont.)

6. **Draw a picture. In your picture, make a dike. Show the sea on one side of the dike. Show the land on the other side. Make sure your land is below sea level in your picture.**

7. *Hot* and *cold* are opposites. Write down the opposites from the story "Sarah and the Giant."

   huge   _____tiny_____   strong   _____

   small   _____   slowly   _____

   Write one or more sentences that tell what each story is about.

8. **"A Country Below Sea Level"** _____

   _____

   _____

9. **"Sarah and the Giant"** _____

   _____

   _____

10. **Tell about where you live. Are you below sea level or above sea level? Are you close to the sea? Are there any dams or dikes near you?**

    _____

    _____

    _____

Bibliography

Barlas, Robert and Norman Tompsett. *Canada*. Gareth Stevens Publishing, 1998.

Betancourt, Jeanne. *Ten True Animal Rescues.* Scholastic, Inc., 1998.

Biel, Timothy Levi. *Zoobooks: Tigers.* Wildlife Education, Ltd., 1992.

Blashfield, Jean F. *Norway.* Children's Press, Grolier Publishing Co., Inc., 2000.

Bockenhauer, Mark H. and Stephen F. Cunha. *Our Fifty States.* National Geographic Society, 2004.

Foster, Ruth. *Down to Earth Geography: Grade 4.* Teacher Created Resources, 2008.

Gibbs Davis, Kathryn. *Wackiest White House Pets.* Scholastic Press, 2004.

Gorrell, Gena K. *Working Like a Dog: The Story of Working Dogs Through History.* Tundra Books, 2003.

Herzog, Brad. *Dare To Be Different: Athletes who Changed Sports.* Sports Illustrated for Kids Books, The Rosen Publishing Group Inc., 2005.

Stepanchuk, Carol. and Charles Wong. *Mooncakes and Hungry Ghosts: Festivals of China.* China Books & Periodicals, Inc., 1991.

Take Five Minutes: Fascinating Facts About Geography. Teacher Created Resources, Inc., 2003.

Take Five Minutes: Fascinating Facts and Stories for Reading and Critical Thinking. Teacher Created Resources, Inc., 2001.

Bibliography (cont.)

Wexo, John Bonnett. *Zoobooks: Animal Wonders.* Wildlife Education, Ltd., 1993.

———. *Zoobooks: Camels.* Wildlife Education, Ltd., 1989.

———. *Zoobooks: Koalas.* Wildlife E ducation, Ltd., 1988.

———. *Zoobooks: Penguins.* Wildlife Education, Ltd., 1988.

———. *Zoobooks: Sharks.* Wildlife Education, Ltd., 1988.

Wulffson, Don L. *The Kid who Invented the Popsicle and Other Surprising Stories About Inventions.* Cobblehill Books, 1997.

Answer Key

Unit 1
1. B
2. B
3. C
4. D
6. 1—Person went to beach;
   3—Person put clams in bucket;
   5—Dog put nose right by bucket and barked.
7. 1st—Sally; 2nd—Sally's brother; 3rd—lady at the other end of the beach

Unit 2
1. D
2. C
3. A
4. D
6. July 20, 1969
7. what: jump high; where: Moon Base 6; when: she is outside the station; why: the moon has less gravity

Unit 3
1. D
2. C
3. B
4. A
6. picture one: person; picture two: koala
7. pizza; pizza; pizza

Unit 4
1. B
2. C
3. D
4. D
6. 1500s: no; no
   1600s: no; yes (pouches)

1700s: yes; yes
today: yes; yes
7. the outside

Unit 5
1. D
2. B
3. C
4. A
6. Hot lava flows out; The hard lava makes new land.
7. *way:* water, snow; *where:* beach, top slopes Mauna Kea; *what:* bathing suit, coat

Unit 6
1. C
2. B
3. B
4. A
6. pony; White House; President Theodore Roosevelt
7. 2,5,4,1,3

Unit 7
1. C
2. B
3. A
4. D
6. 2,1; 1,2
7. 3,4,1,2; Scott, Morgan, Morgan, Scott

Unit 8
1. D
2. B
3. A
4. C
6. father=bull; baby=calf
7. Kim went to the country; Betty told Kim she was looking at cows.

Answer Key (cont.)

Unit 9
1. C
2. B
3. A
4. A
6. 1—Pacific; 2—Atlantic; 3—Indian; 4—Arctic
7. all colors should be circled

Unit 10
1. A
2. B
3. C
4. D
6. print—B; tiger—C
7. 3,4,1,2; May, Lee, May, Lee

Unit 11
1. D
2. B
3. D
4. A
6. eyes-see; fingers-feel
7. 4,3,2,1; Zack, Uncle Henry, Uncle Henry, Zack

Unit 12
1. C
2. D
3. A
4. B
6. *first shape*—combination of: Andrea was buried up to her chest; Andrea was blown into a bank of snow; *last shape*—combination of: Villa heard Andrea and jumped over fence; Andrea held onto Villa, and Villa pulled her out.

Unit 13
1. B   2. C   B. D   4. A

6. an ocean: a lake; can: cannot; above: below
7. egg in fresh water should be at bottom of glass; egg in salty water should be floating

Unit 14
1. D
2. B
3. C
4. A
6. city: plowed roads, cars and trucks; country: unplowed roads, sleighs and horses
7. 2,4,3,1; nurse, nurse, doctor, doctor

Unit 15
1. A
2. B
3. C
4. D
7. Greeting: Dear Franklin, Closing: Your pen pal from Bahrain, Ali

Unit 16
1. C
2. B
3. A
4. D
6. A
7. *like a boat:* floats; *not like a boat:* made up of animals joined together, rolls in and out of the water

Unit 17
1. A   3. B
2. D   4. C
6. pitching with his one hand; throwing with his one hand
7. left, right, right, left

Answer Key (cont.)

Unit 18
1. C
2. A
3. C
4. D
6. play games; have fun; talk; laugh; set off firecrackers
7. *light:* lit a big bonfire; *noise:* lit firecrackers; *red:* painted the doors of their homes

Unit 19
1. D
2. B
3. B
4. C
6. *shark:* more, more, faster
   you: less, less, slower
7. *before:* Hoon had two loose teeth, or Hoon wiggled his teeth with his tongue;
   after: Hoon could not find his teeth, or Hoon's teeth got stuck in the apple, or Hoon's father and sister came running.

Unit 20
1. C
2. B
3. C
4. D
6. *stars:* white, 50
   field: blue, 1
   stripes: red and white; 13
7. school, library, fire station, police station

Unit 21
1. A
2. D
3. D
4. B
6. It was too cold; There was no one to help on the way.
7. 4,2,1,5,3; Jon, Jon, Ryan, Ryan, Ryan

Unit 22
1. D
2. C
3. A
4. A
6. 1; 2; 0, 1, or 2 (with fingers)
7. 4,2,1,5,3

Unit 23
1. A
2. B
3. D
4. A
6. Answer could be a mix of—
   First Box: wind is strong, water is choppy, ships told not to cross the channel, Gertrude swims in choppy channel water;
   Third Box: Gertrude stays in the water, Gertrude swims across the channel, Gertrude is first woman to swim from France to England.
7. (August) 5 (or 6) 2008

Unit 24
1. D   2. A   3. B   4. C
7. no, yes, no, yes, yes

Unit 25
1. C   2. D   3. A   4. B
7. big, weak, faster